BigTime® Piano

Disney

EL 4

Arranged by Nancy and Randall Faber

This book belongs to: _____

Production Coordinator: Jon Ophoff
Editor: Isabel Otero Bowen
Design and Illustration: Terpstra Design, San Francisco
Engraving: Dovetree Productions, Inc.

FABER
PIANO ADVENTURES®

HAL•LEONARD®

A NOTE TO TEACHERS

BigTime® Piano Disney brings together contemporary and classic Disney hits arranged for the Level 4 pianist and beyond. In the words of Walt Disney, "There is more treasure in books than in all the pirates' loot on Treasure Island." This book offers musical treasure for piano students with blockbusters from *Aladdin, Beauty and the Beast, The Hunchback of Notre Dame, The Lion King, Moana, Mulan,* and more.

BigTime® Piano is part of the PreTime to BigTime Supplementary Piano Library arranged by Faber & Faber. The series allows students to enjoy a favorite style at their current level of study.

BigTime books are available in the following styles: Christmas, Classics, Disney, Favorites, Hits, Hymns, Kids' Songs, Popular, Ragtime & Marches, Rock 'n Roll, and the Faber Studio Collection—offering a sampling of many styles.

Visit us at **PianoAdventures.com**.

Helpful Hints:

1. The songs can be assigned in any order. Selection is usually best made by the student, according to interest and enthusiasm.

2. Hands-alone practice is often helpful. Ensure that the playing is rhythmic even in hands-alone practice.

3. As rhythm is of prime importance, encourage the student to feel the rhythm in his or her body when playing. This can be accomplished with the tapping of the toe or heel, and with clapping exercises.

THE PRETIME TO BIGTIME PIANO LIBRARY

PreTime® Piano	=	Primer Level
PlayTime® Piano	=	Level 1
ShowTime® Piano	=	Level 2A
ChordTime® Piano	=	Level 2B
FunTime® Piano	=	Level 3A–3B
BigTime® Piano	=	Level 4 & above

ISBN 978-1-61677-722-7

Printed in U.S.A.

TABLE OF CONTENTS

We Know the Way

from *MOANA*

Music by OPETAIA FOA'I
Lyrics by OPETAIA FOA'I
and LIN-MANUEL MIRANDA

Strong, moderate beat

6

*For smaller hands, the lower G may be omitted.

Can You Feel the Love Tonight

from *The Lion King*

Music by ELTON JOHN
Lyrics by TIM RICE

An en-chant - ed mo - ment,___ and it sees___ me through.
There's a rhyme___ and rea - son___ to the wild___ out - doors.

It's e-nough___ for this rest-less war-rior just to be___ with you. And___
When the heart___ of this star-crossed voyag-er beats in time___ with yours.

can you feel___ the love___ to - night?___

It is where___ we are.

It's e-nough___ for this wide - eyed___ wan-der-er that we've got this far.

Be Prepared

from *The Lion King*

Music by ELTON JOHN
Words by TIM RICE

FF3055

Dig a Little Deeper

from *The Princess and the Frog*

Music and Lyrics by
RANDY NEWMAN

Cadenza, freely

Alice in Wonderland

from *ALICE IN WONDERLAND*

Words by BOB HILLIARD
Music by SAMMY FAIN

Moderate jazz waltz, with rubato

FF3055

I'll Make a Man Out of You

from *Mulan*

Music by MATTHEW WILDER
Lyrics by DAVID ZIPPEL

Moderato, energetic

Let's get down to bus - 'ness___ to de -
Tran - quil as a for - est,___ but on

feat the Huns.___
fire with - in.___

Did they send me daugh - ters___ when I
Once you find your cen - ter___ you are

asked for sons?___ You're the
sure to win.___ You're a

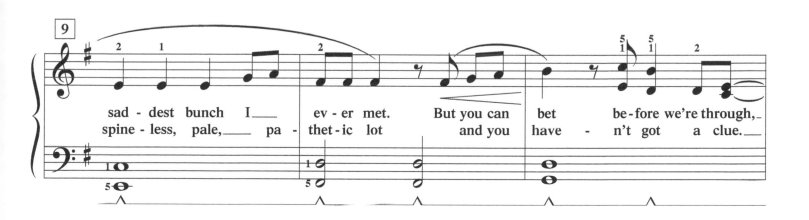

sad - dest bunch I____ ev - er met. But you can bet be - fore we're through,____
spine - less, pale,____ pa - thet - ic lot and you have - n't got a clue.____

Mis - ter, I'll____ make a man____ out of you.____
Some-how I'll____ make a man____

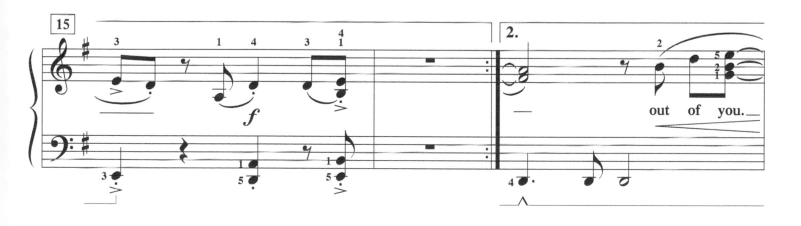

out of you.____

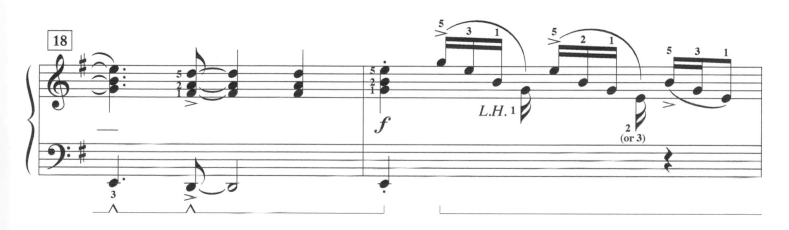

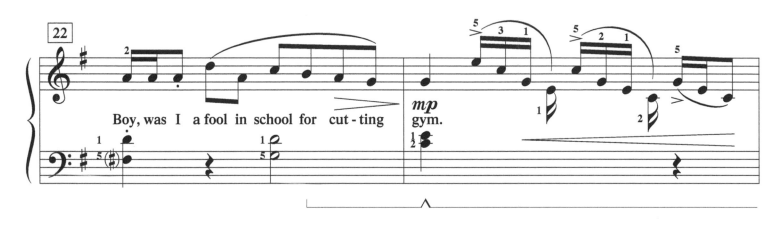

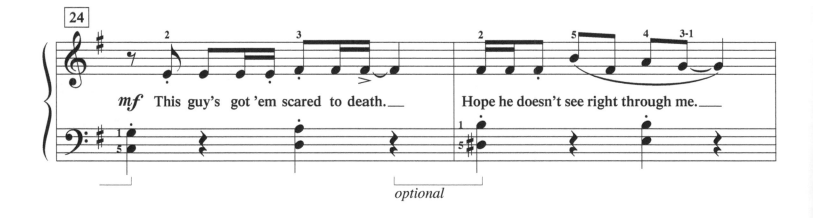

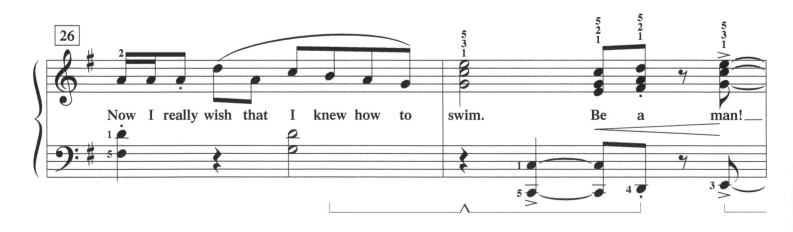

Just Around the Riverbend

from *POCAHONTAS*

Music by ALAN MENKEN
Lyrics by STEPHEN SCHWARTZ

26

FF3055

Two Worlds

from *TARZAN*®

Words and Music by
PHIL COLLINS

FF3055

28

Aladdin Medley

from *ALADDIN*

Music by ALAN MENKEN
Lyrics by HOWARD ASHMAN
Except * Lyrics by TIM RICE

32

Friend Like Me
Moderate swing

FF3055

34

A Whole New World*

God Help the Outcasts

from *The Hunchback of Notre Dame*

Music by ALAN MENKEN
Lyrics by STEPHEN SCHWARTZ

38

luck - y than I. Please help my

peo - ple, the poor and down - trod.

I thought we all were the chil - dren of

God. God help the out - casts

chil - dren of God.

Beauty and the Beast

from *BEAUTY AND THE BEAST*

Music by ALAN MENKEN
Lyrics by HOWARD ASHMAN

42

Prologue

from *Beauty and the Beast*

Music by ALAN MENKEN

48